Augusta Cleveland Prindle

Alpine Flowers

And Other Poems

Augusta Cleveland Prindle

Alpine Flowers
And Other Poems

ISBN/EAN: 9783744711081

Printed in Europe, USA, Canada, Australia, Japan

Cover: Foto ©Thomas Meinert / pixelio.de

More available books at **www.hansebooks.com**

ALPINE FLOWERS,

AND

OTHER POEMS,

BY

AUGUSTA CLEVELAND PRINDLE.

AUTHOR "OF PAST, PRESENT AND FUTURE," "WHITE LILIES," AUNT ELSIE'S
STORY," "DECORATION DAY," ETC., ETC.

———— • • • ————

SPRINGFIELD, MASS.:
WHITNEY & ADAMS,
1879.

TO

THE MEMORY OF MY DEPARTED

MOTHER,

T. ARETHUSA DAVISON CLEVELAND,

Whose patience, resignation and piety were my admiration;
Whose love, counsel and encouragement were my inspiration,

" ALPINE FLOWERS, "

WHICH ARE AN EMBLEM OF HER LIFE,

IS

AFFECTIONATELY DEDICATED

BY

THE AUTHOR.

CONTENTS.

ALPINE FLOWERS.

AMID the Alps eternal snows
  Alone the Alpine flowers bloom,
Content, that, thus near Heaven's gate
  They dwell in grandeur and in gloom.

The mountain bares its lofty brow
  And to its bosom tempts the storm ;
But in its chink of rifted snow,
  The floweret rests secure and warm.

'Tis born of storms, and swathed in snow,
  Its nutriment keen, frosted air :
Yet fairer, sweeter, purer flowers
  Not sunny vales can claim or wear.

Its tiny petals never boast

The brilliant hues exotics wear,

Nor pungent odors scent the breeze

With fragrance crypt in anthers rare.

Yet that which forms her meed of good

Received from Nature's lavish hand,   `

Without reserve she freely gives

As tribute to a weary land.

But thousands bud and bloom and fade

Unseen save by their Maker's eye ;

Their mission is not mine to solve,—

They lived for God,—for Him they die.

The traveler struggling with the storm,

Or basking in the sun's bright beams,

Will stop to cull the fragile flowers ;—

Will weave their sweetness in his dreams,

Will mingle them with far-off homes,—
　　With bright eyes watching far away,—
With busy fingers—rosy lips—
　　With priest, and bride, and marriage day.

Will smiling view their azure tint—
　　Their purity so sweet and rare ;
Will strive to make his life as pure
　　As far from pride, as nobly fair.

Once on a time when Love was young,
　　An eagle caught him in his mirth,
Its talons fastened round his heart,
　　And bore him, bleeding, from the earth.

But as they crossed the Alpine crest
　　The last drops left his wounded side,
And from these sprang the Alpine flowers,
　　Not red—but fair and azure dyed.

And, pendant from each rootlet small,
There glows a ruby rich,—so rare
No prince can buy,—and none but these,
. The pure in heart, may own, or wear.

Earth ne'er had claimed a child so pure
The Alpine rubies it could wear,—
And when convulsed with Calvary's throes
They fused with Love incarnate there.

And true love blending with divine,
Evolved rich jewels fine and rare,—
The " Pearl of price," and starry crowns
Which only those redeemed can wear.

Nor wear them here where eyes are dimmed
With tears evoked by sorrow's power,
Where conquest still is unachieved,
Where strife and conflict are our dower.

But just beyond the mystic stream
  Whose waters lave life's either shore,
Shall conquerers, crowned by Love divine,
  Reflect His glory evermore.

'Twas Alpine Flowers inspired my song,
  They are the wand which wakes my lyre,
On avalanche and glacier's brow
  Their petals glow with poet's fire.

I strive to catch the glowing flame,—
  To bind Pegasus to my car ;
He hurries on the trackless way,
  The lucid light recedes afar.

All, all alone ! The hand of Fate
  Points sternly down the lonely way;
With trembling step, and blanching cheek,
  I bow in silence, and obey.

In darknesss, weary, sad, alone,
  Upon the mountain pass I stand,
A gleaner mid the chilling storm,—
  A gleaner's harvest in my hand.

A *gleaner*? Ah, what have we here?
  A flower of patience dearly bought,—
A bit of hearts-ease frail as fair,—
  A spray of Love's forget-me-not,—

A faded, broken, laurel wreath,—
  A cross with sweetest hopes entwined,—
A tiny blade of golden grain,
  Perchance, amid the sheaf we find,—

The distant murmur of a song,—
  The breathings of a magic lute,—
The memory of a whispered vow,—
  The echo of a voice now mute.

These are the gleanings from the storm
And aptly christened Alpine Flowers,
And, like that mountain flower, they fade
Transplanted to earth's sunny bowers.

We do not proffer them to those
Who cull from Flora's fragrant bowers,
For rich exotics do not find
A rival in our Alpine Flowers.

If words expressed from saddened hearts
To bless sad hearts alone have power,
Then may some suffering one here glean
A spray to garland sorrow's hour.

'Twas she who sang their natal song,
When grief and woe announced their birth,
Wrung from the bleeding heart of love,—
Nursed by the chilling frosts of earth.

2

The subtle alchemy of frost
That massive boulders breaks in twain,
Doth gently ope the forest mast,
And shade and verdure grace the plain.

So bitter grief, like winter's frost,
Doth crack the shell of selfish hearts,
Reveals the tiny germ of love,
Which .to vicarious being starts.—

Starts onward nerved to deeds sublime,
Expanding as its branches rise ;
Thus blessed and blessing till it finds
Its home perennial in the skies.

Sorrows are germs for higher life,
From which great natures may evolve
Rich gems of thought, as center suns
Round which grand principles revolve.

The gems evolved by chemic art
From sorrow, trial, grief and tears,
And crystallized on Calvary's brow,
Shall brighter glow through countless years.

And He whom Justice bleeding bore
Aloft o'er Calvary's rugged height,
Bedecked its brow with gems so rare
That earth and heaven reflect their light.

Before their glorious rays the sun
Shall veil its face in darkest night,
And Calvary's bleeding victim prove
The light of life, and life of light.

NEARER.

"NEARER my God to thee" through hours
    Thy love doth grant in sunny bowers,
Or if the shadowing cross I see
My cry will still be nearer thee.

So near to thee that every cross
Will prove a crucible for dross,
And every grief and trial be
But waves to bear me nearer thee.

Nearer to thee while life shall last,
Nearer to thee.when death is past;
In heaven still my cry shall be,
Dear Saviour, keep me nearer thee.

No angel bowing round thy throne
Hath such delight thy love to own :
The love that gave thy life for me
Will surely keep me near to thee.

2*

OLD AGE.

"Man goeth to his long home."

YES, journeying onward with no thought of rest
   From the toils and the trials by which we are
      pressed,
Through sorrow and sadness, through sunshine and
   gloom,
We know, just before us, our goal is the tomb.

The sun now shines dimly, the moon disappears,
And the stars seem like hopes of the far away years,
While the clouds of spent anguish in sorrow we view,
Are gathering round our bowed spirit anew.

The windows are draped, and the deepest of gloom
Pervades, all unbidden, the dark, cheerless room,
Where Fancy reads backwards from Memory's tome
Of years that have vanished, of friends who are gone.

The birds singing anthems of praise at our door,

We deem but the voices of loved ones of yore,

We join in the chorus with tremulous glee,

And the songsters, affrighted, decamp from the tree.

In the shade of the flourishing almond we wait

For the angel to open the beautiful gate ;

In rapture we sing as we view the bright dome

Of the city of God and our glorified home.

So fainting and weary we long for its rest,

Fair earth let us hide in thy sheltering breast ;

In thy green curtained chambers there surely is room

For a pale, quiet tenant to find a long home.

*   *   *   *   *   *   *   *

Now close the door softly and curtain our bed,

For sweetly we 'll sleep where the daisies are spread

Until that bright morning when Jesus will come

To waken the sleeping, and welcome them home.

THIRTY-THREE.

ELEVEN times one are eleven,—
                    O fly
Ye years; do not tarry, I'm longing to try
My powers in the conflict,—my voice in the song
That gladdens the warriors while fighting the wrong.
I've cared for the Baby, and Eddie, and Lou,
I heard you tell Auntie, quite equal to you;
But I guess that. my body's too young for my soul,
For I find *that* the hardest of all to control.
'Twill soar like the eagle away to the sun —
Then question to know when the morning stars sung?
And you say I am *dreaming* when I'm seeking to know
Why that promise to Noah was sealed with a bow.

Eleven times two are twenty-two,—
                    Away in the West
New England's own daughter is striving her best

To rescue the erring, to silence the wrong,

To cheer the faint-hearted and weary with song;

Her spirit aspiring, and scorning earth's rest,

Would gather rich sheaves for the home of the blest,

Bnt the voice of the Master bade " suffer," " be still,"—

And in loving submission she bowed to his will ;

Thus waiting, and watching, and wandering lone,

Each heart-throb a prayer, and each prayer but a moan,

She measures the years, which, though dark they may
    gleam,

Still thrill with the echo of youth's brightest dream.

Eleven times three are thirty-three.

They sped—

The years, but she garnered bright gems as they fled,—

The brightest from sorrow, the largest from pain,

And her diamonds are crystallized tear-drops of rain,

From the chiseling hand of the Sculptor she stands

A statue, awaiting his farther command,

Nor care if the mansion, or quarry retain

The work, which, in either, his glory proclaim.

The thirty-third link of the lengthening chain

Of the years, she 's been clasping to-day without pain ;

For Hope, the bright minstrel which springs from the
  throne,

Is thrilling her soul with sweet music of home.

A CLOVER BLOSSOM.

WHY did I cull you from your bed?
 You bloomed in beauty there,
I thought to cheer a lonely hour
With your sweet face so fair.

But even you a thorn conceal,
You mock me with the past,
You whisper of those happy hours
Of youth, too bright to last.—

When skipping lightly o'er the lawn,
I culled the flowers which grew
Around my path, but, gentle one
I crowned my friends with you.

You speak of hopes that once were bright
And fresh with morning dew,
Ere I had learned deception's power
Or found the world untrue.

The stone from Memory's door you've rolled,
And youth's loved friends are near,
Who long since traversed streets of gold,
And left the wanderer here,—

So lonely that to-night I yearn
For one bright gleam of bliss,
From their blest home, to strengthen me
To bear the ills of this.

I gaze into thy sunny face,
A gleam of hope is there;
" The morning star, you say, will rise,
The shadows disappear ;—

The glorious dawn will usher in
A day supremely blest,
When not a doubt or grief shall mar
The glory of thy rest."

3

LIGHT AT EVENING.

"At evening time it shall be light."

LIGHT at evening!—blessed promise
  That life's darkest storms shall flee,—
That each bitter cloud of sorrow
  Shall but bright reflectors be
Of the radiance which shall hover
  Round the spirits evening time,
Singing lullabys of heaven
  Which with angel harpings chime.

In the morn of life the sunbeams
  Flooded all our path with light,
But the noontime found the tempest
  Draping the same path in night.

Then, amid the muttering thunders,
  Lo, a gentle voice we hear :—
" Hope and trust,—beyond these shadows
  Shall the evening light appear."

Almost o'er our pilgrim journey,
  Grief and trials almost o'er,
Wistfully we watch the shadows
  Which above our spirit soar,—
Watching for the golden glimmer
  Which will banish sorrow's night,—
Waiting for the blessed promise—
  "Lo, at evening cometh light."

THE VISION.

I HAD a vision strangely bright,
  A vision, blending earth with heaven,
So gently, that I never deemed
  The mystic veil was still unriven.

I mingled with the ransomed throng;
  My lyre, immortal, chimed with their's;
My voice exultant joined the song
  Which rose sublime from myriad choirs.

The throng, adoring, cast their crowns
  In homage at the Savior's feet;
'Twas then I saw that mine alone
  Of all that band was incomplete.

No jewel sparkled on its crest
  Reflecting radiance from the throne ;
I stood among the garnered sheaves
  Redeemed, but with a starless crown.

I felt I had no right to share
  The joys to faithful laborers given ;
Their crowns were bright with many stars,—
  Saved souls they'd won from vice to heaven.

The vision changed, I turned away
  In sorrow from the happy throng,
And earthward did my footsteps tend,
  Fraught with a mission, noble, strong.

I saw the ripened harvest spread
  Wide as the world, the reapers few ;
I joined the number, and with joy
  Did glean till eve brought star and dew.
  3*

I shunned no path the Savior led ;
     Faith was my guide, my refuge prayer ;
I sought among the haunts of vice,
     And found my brightest jewels there.

Again the mystic scene is changed,
     Again with saints in heaven I bow ;
I do not mind my crown or stars,
     For Jesus has my homage now.

In joy I cast it at his feet,
     His love hath set its every gem
Firm and eternal as the stars
     Which sparkle in his diadem.

THE WATCHER.

A WATCHER lone at Memory's gate,
   I silent view the passing throng,
Whose footsteps time my heart's quick throb,
   Whose voiceless greeting haunts me long.

I join the moving, motley crowd,
   As back toward cradle-time they press;
I tread life's later weary years
   To find its spring-time love and rest.

I drink again life's cup of joy,
   I revel in its peaceful dream,
Nor look for storms when skies are fair,
   Or quicksands in so pure a stream.

But vain the dream of tranquil seas
   On which my flower 'decked barge would glide,
Freighted with choicest, richest store,
   Make heaven's port on rising tide.

Again I meet the loved, the lost ;—
   Again love's accents thrill mine ears,—
Again forget what love has cost,
   And that its dower is nought but tears.

There pass the loved of later days,
   But life still young, and hope *so* bright,—
Those vanished, these too passed away,
   And left but faith for beacon light.

I wistful gaze among the throng
   For one 't were long since sin to know,
I catch one last, fond, lingering glance,
   As, fair and sad, she glides along.

THE WATCHER.

My spirit bowed beneath the view
 As erst it did when hope expired ;
Had hope expired? Ah! late I knew
 That it had only been deferred.

Be brave my heart! thou still must wear
 A mask to hide thy every throb,
Till death, less cruel than is deemed,
 Unveil thee at the bar of God.

Ah, while I wait the tableau changed,
 Changed rapid as life's fleeting dream,
I only see the phantom shades
 Pass slowly down life's narrow stream.

I weary of my lonely watch—
 I step inside of Memory's gate,
Bid Hope give Faith her useless key ;
 And only ask for grace to wait.—

Wait Heaven's illuminating ray,

    The *wherefore* of this weary road—

The promise that I then shall know

    Why sorrow only leads to God.

LONGING FOR HOME.

LONGING for home. 'Tis just over the River,
  The River so narrow, the glimmer I see
 Of its bright, pearly gates, its mansions eternal
 Where loved ones, with Jesus, are waiting for me

Waiting they watch me as onward I hasten,
  Hastening onward I wait on the strand,
 Watching the ebb-tide, to bear my barque over
  Death's surging wave to the glorified land.

Home of my soul! Not long would I linger
  A stranger and pilgrim away from the fold,
 Shepherd, O, list to the cry of the wanderer,
  Rescue thy lamb from the pitiless cold.

Weary and faint, nought but thorns for my pillow,

  Dark gleams the past and the present to me,

My future resplendent with glory is beaming,

  Oh, mother and heaven, I 'm longing for thee.

" Not *yet* " can I enter those bright hallowed portals,

  Then patience impart—let no murmur arise,

Gird me with strength in thy vineyard to labor ;

  Be duty my pleasure—Thy glory my prize.

Longing for home !   Ah, tear-drops are falling,

  Poor heart, wilt thou never prove stronger and brave ?

Hush thy impatience, thy home thou art nearing,

  Haste, forth to the harvest, seek others to save.

Now quiet my spirit, in patience I linger ;

  Silenced each longing, but waiting *so* lone,

While Faith points the way with her glory-tipped finger,

  Where Jesus and mother make heaven and home.

I am learning to wait, as I stand by the River,

  Still waiting to learn a kind Father's behest;

Soon shall I list to the oar of the ferryman

  Sent by compassion to bear me to rest.

4

HEREAFTER.

" What I do thou knowest not now, but thou shalt know hereafter."

I KNOW not why the cherished dreams
  Which gladdened childhood's happy morn
Must need have felt the chilling blight
  Which blasts the rose but spares its thorn.

I know not why a faithless world
  With nought but thorns would crown my brow,
Nor why the friends the most beloved,
  To death's stern mandate soonest bow.

I know not why the goddess Love
  Did thrill my soul with mystic power,
Awoke such sweet and joyous hopes
  To blight and wither in an hour.

I know not why this aching heart
    Must bear its load of grief alone,—
Must hush each hope of joy, and long
    For angel hands to bear me home.

Ah, there I'll know why I have drank
    This cup of bitter sorrow here,
With joy will reap the harvest which
    Was sown in grief, and wet with tears.

I'll not despair,—a Father's hand
    Will not inflict a needless blow,
And if his ways I cannot trace
    He says, " Hereafter thou shalt know,"—

" Shall know why I have led thee through
    Dark scenes of trial and distress ;
And brought thee, purified by woe
    To heaven thy everlasting rest."

TO MOTHER.

MOTHER sleep sweetly. Thou hast won
A pearl wreath :—An immortal crown
Reflects the light from yonder throne,
Thou knowest the joys of heaven thine own.

Hast thou an angel's lovely form,
Sent forth to comfort those who mourn?
O, come and lull the grief most wild,
Which racks the bosom of thy child.

And as in sorrow, grief, and fears,
Thou didst pass through this vale of tears,
Pity thy child, and ease the smart
Of my poor, wounded, aching heart.

Thou sure hast known the bitter woe,
Through which thy weary child must go—
The tears of blood which I have shed,
Since thou hast slumbered with the dead.

O, could I, as in days of yore,
My grief into thy bosom pour,
Thy loving smile would cheer my heart,
Thy soothing words bid grief depart.

Mother, dear mother, come to-night,
Draw back the curtain. let the light
From yonder throne transfuse my soul,
And make my bleeding heart-wounds whole.

Ah! now, yes *now*, I feel thee near,
Hush earthly discord while I hear
The voice which gently tells the way
Which leads to heaven's unclouded day.—

" Your Savior drank the cup of woe,

You tread the path he led below,

To him, triumphant on his throne,   .

God leadeth you by paths unknown.

" Press on through sorrow, grief and fears,

Eternal love awards your tears,

Do not despair, or yield to gloom,

Eternal life springs from the tomb.

" My child, remember that each tear

You shed in woe is garnered here,

For *you* the only way to Heaven

Must be through sorrows He has given.

ONWARD AND UPWARD.

ONWARD, for the goal's above thee;
    Wherefore loiter by the way?
None but cowards faint and falter;
    Gird thy loins, and haste away,

Upward, for the mount is glowing,
    Beams translucent fill the air;
Strive, and thou shalt gain its summit,
    Upward toil, and bravely dare.

· Onward, lo, a glorious future
    Gleams beyond the opening door;
Bravely rend each bolt asunder
    And reveal its hidden lore;—

Science stands within the portal
    Crowned by Hope with chaplets rare,
And all those who bravely enter
    Shall a crown of laurel wear.

Onward! see the bondmen's shackles *
    Falling in oblivion's shade,—
Free Columbia proudly soaring
    From the pestilential glade.

Upward, on untiring pinion,
    See her eagle on the wing,
Till, the climax gained, triumphant
    Victory's song she'll sweetly sing.

Onward, never yield the contest,
    Sow the seeds of light and love,
In the soil o'errun with error,
    And await the fruit above.

* Written during the late Civil War.

Onward, in the path of duty ;
  Upward, still thy constant song,
Till, in heaven crowned with glory
  Thou hast joined the ransomed throng.

LINES.

"AH who is there but that would fain
　　Become a child once more
If future years would bring again
　　All that they brought before."—

Landon.

Backward? No! onward let me press
　　To conflict, conquest, crown,
The past has been misfortune's claim,
　　The future's all my own.

What? backward to those parting scenes—
　　Those hours of bitter woe—
Which flood the soul with sorrow's power—
　　Oh, *wherefore*, should I go?

To quaff again the cup of woe
  Which once my lips hath pressed
Would rob the future of its charm,
  The present of its rest.

What if the sun on life did cast
  In youth, a few bright beams ;
'Twere not enough to tempt my feet
  To walk again its streams.

I would my trembling barque urge on
  To the deep sea of life,
'Tis near the coast the shoals abound—
  The rocks and dangers rife.

I know the future may be dark,
  Its skies be chill and drear,
But through the gloaming Faith is seen ;
  And Heaven's port I near.

Then on, I'll hasten to the goal,
  Nor linger longer here,
For Heaven hath balm for every wound,
  And dries the mourner's tear.

Soon life will dawn upon my soul,
  And there no blight is known,—
The Present and the Future meet
  And mingle round the Throne.

"IS IT WELL WITH THE CHILD?"

IS it well with the child? Has it laved in the fountain

I opened for sin when I bled on the tree?
I've sought it, I've called it—I've died to redeem it,—
In childhood, Oh, guide its young footsteps to me!

On the mountains of sin 'tis not well it should wan-
der

An alien from God, and a stranger to grace,
No pleasures hath earth like the joy of my favor,—
No rest but my sheltering haven of grace.

'Tis well with the children, if, crowding my pathway
The arms of my love doth enfold them once more;

5

I'll lead and support them through joys and through
    sorrow,
  And bring them through grace to the glorified shore ;

To the home of their Savior where anthems are ringing,
  Where palm branches wave, and the ransomed rejoice,
Where praises to Jesus the children are singing,
  With no cadence of sorrow enthrilling their voice.

THE CONFLICT.

WEARY of earth, O, Father grant repose
    In the full fountain of thy matchless love ;
O, give the quiet which from Thee descends
    Blest token that with thine, my soul doth blend !

Rugged the path amid the tangled thorns,
    And long the way to pilgrim's weary feet,
My strength is gone ; loud roars the angry storm,
    Impart thy strength and crown thy grace complete.

I am so weary of the aimless strife,—
    The souls fierce struggle 'gainst its prison bars ;—
The fruitless longing for a higher life,—
    The countless errors which my spirit mars.

Earth hath no balm for aching, suffering hearts,
  Nor panacea for the mind's unrest,
Her only lethean fountain is the grave ;—
  Her only hope assurance of its rest.

To-night I fain would rise above the world,
  And catch from angel lips some sweet refrain,
Whose inspiration quelling every fear,
  Shall fit me wholly for the martyr's pain.

The martyr's pain? Ah, there are other fires,
  (Which purify the soul from earthly dross),
Than those which bore in chariots of fire,
  A mighty throng to glory from the cross.

For martyrs traverse still earth's Calvaries,
  And crowns of thorns are pressed on many brows;
We see the crown, they feel the piercing thorn,
  And sing their sweetest songs in saddest hours.

Their sweetest songs! Ah! angels only know
  The anguished throes which call them into birth;
Aye, blood and tears unite to form the song
  Which lures to Heaven a sorrowing child of earth.

Amid the fires a pæon would I raise
  To Him who kindles for my good the flame;
I raise the song, He floods my soul with praise
  My weary soul is laving in the fount of love.

Earth and its trials are beneath my feet;
  Its thorns all changed to amaranthine flowers,
The victor's crown is sparkling on my brow;
  The conqueror's song, exultant, claims the hour.

    5*

GENIUS AWAKING.

THE slumbering genius of the soul
   Must now arise, assert its power;
Too long unmindful of its goal,
   It slept within a rosy bower.

But now a voice in thunder tone
   Doth call "Come forth," she heeds the cry,
As angel hands remove the stone,
   She plumes her wings and soars on high.

By slumber now no more inthralled
   She rose, and, with a conqueror's tread,
Quick from her throne the vassal hurled,
   And placed the crown on her own head.

She quaffs the life-inspiring breeze

    Which gently fans the brow of Fame,

Who twines a wreath of laurel leaves,

    Which shed their fragrance round her name.

Clothed like the sun in robes of light

    No lesser orb she seeks to dim,

For as they bask in borrowed rays,

    She boasts reflection too from him.

MOLLIE PITCHER.

.

"The heroine of Monmouth, June 28, 1778. Her husband, an artillery-man, was shot, and fell dead just as she was carrying him some water. She heard his commander order the gun from the field, and hastened to it and faithfully performed her husband's duty until night closed the contest."—Hist.

DEAR Mollie, come not here again,
   Too great the risk you run,
This is no place for such as you,
   Go! I must mind the gun.

No place for such as me? John, know
   My country's foes are mine,
If duty calls thee to the front
   It calls me next in line.

Here, take this luncheon, and this draught
  Of water from the spring,
And while you rest your weary self,
  I 'll make the valleys ring.

She took his place beside the gun;
  He rested in its shade;
And while he ate, its brazen tongue
  Resounded through the glade.

Again, and yet again, until
  Refreshed he 's by her side.
"Please let me stay, dear John," she plead,
  "No harm will me betide."

No, darling, go! The foe so strong
  May make our numbers yield,
The battle o'er, I 'll go to you
  To-night across the field.

A kiss, a blessing, and they part,
　　When will their meeting be?
Across the fields?　Ah, yes, of life!
　　"To-night?"—*eternity.*

But long she cannot stay away,
　　Again she fills her pail,
And as she nears her husband's side,
　　Strength, hope and courage fail,—

For reeling from the gun he falls,—
　　He falls, nor falls alone!
"My God," she cries, "O, take me too,
　　"Oh, let me, too, go home!"

"Home to our Father's house on high—
　　"Where war is aye unknown,
"Spare me life's long and weary road;
　　"My Father, take me home!"

While agonizing thus she lay
A voice sounds in her ear,—
" Remove this cannon from the field,—
" The gunner 's fallen here."

An inspiration thrills her soul,
She hastens to the gun,
And bravely fills her husband's place
Till victory is won.

The dear dead lying by her side
Thrilled every nerve with power,
Her *duty* could not wait, but *grief*—
Ah, grief should have her hour.

Ah, who can tell the grief which wrung
Her woman's heart so true,
As, gazing on her pallid dead,
She strove his task to do.

His task and hers! Their country's need

   A holocaust demands,

She felt the easier task were his

   Who slept with folded hands.

THE WEDDING.

I HEARD the chime of merry bells
    Upon thy lovely bridal morn,
I saw them wreathe thy bride's fair brow
    With flowers which innocence adorn.

I saw the fair and gentle girl
    Lean trustingly upon thy arm,
I heard you lisp those magic words
    Which make of kindred souls, but one.

'Tis well.. Deception's cruèl power
    Hath long since lured me from thy side,
My love lies buried deep in flowers,
    And now, with joy, I greet thy bride.

6

What matter if an aching heart
    I've decked with flowers of brightest hue,
The world doth ever choose to gaze
    Upon a picture fair to view.

My lips I've wreathed in sunny smiles,
    To hide the grief my heart doth bear,
I'll warble songs of hope and cheer,
    To hush the wailing of despair.

Yet once I caught your earnest gaze
    Rest on me fondly as of yore,
I saw—I feared your heart still true ;
    For Eloquence could say no more.

I scarce knew why I left the church·
    And sought our seat beneath the yew,—
Nor why I wept that he who claimed
    My vows, had severed love so true.

God grant thy sea of life may prove
   As tranquil as mine is uneven ;
Sweet thought, the wildest storms but bear
   Us sooner to our rest in Heaven.

Till then farewell ?　Let ne'er a thought
   Of me, intrude within thy home,
But trust in God, for, soon or late
   Our severed hearts will claim their own.

"LILIE MAY."

WEEP not for Lilie, sweetest flower
 That ever graced a parent stem ;
Nor mourn that she, so young, hath gone
 To 'deck the Savior's diadem.

Weep not for her, so bright, so fair,
 Your heart's fond treasure and delight,
For angels gently bore the gem,
 To bask in Heaven's refulgent light.

Weep not for Lilie. Sweet the thought
 That she, an angel presence now,
Hath learned to lisp the song of Heaven,
 Hath learned at Jesus' feet to bow.

She left a world with sorrow rife,
　　Ere yet a thorn had pierced her brow—
Ere yet the bitter cup of woe,
　　Had taught her soul in grief to bow.

Dear parents, weep not that your flower
　　Is gathered from your tender care,
Transplanted to a fairer clime.
　　'Twill bloom in fadeless beauty there.

Then strew with fairest flowers the sod
　　Which holds the casket;—but the gem
In faith and hope resign to God,
　　Assured they will unite again.

Weep not for her!　She sweetly calls
　　For you to meet her in that home
Of rapturous beauty, light and love,—
　　"O, papa, mama, will you come?"

OUR HOPES.

"Bring forth your hopes and look at them."

O WEARY, lonely, suffering heart,
  Where *are* the blissful Hopes *so* dear,
Which, fairy watchers at thy shrine,
  Admitted neither grief nor fear?

With heart elate, I tripped along
  The path of life with joyous tread;
But, ah, too soon I found that thorns
  Blent with the roses round my head.

Too soon I felt a withering blight
  Cast its dark shadow o'er the day,
And at its frown, the voice of Hope
  Chanted a dirge, then fled away.

"Come back! Come back!" I wildly cried,
　"And cheer my darkness with your song:"
The agony she may not view
　Which breaks a heart once brave and strong.

"Bring out your Hopes." If I but had
　One flickering gleam to cheer my way,
'Twere balm to heal my wounded heart,—
　'Twere noon-tide splendor to my day.

"Bring out your Hopes?" Alas, my heart
　I've searched in vain for one bright gleam;
The dark-browed visage of Despair
　Doth haunt me, even in my dream.

Though Hope, for me, is all a blank,
　And earth is clothed in darkest night,
Amid the gloom sweet Faith appears,
　And fills my soul with heavenly light.

The festal robe of white she wears ;

The conqueror's palm is in her hand ;

She gently whispers, " Calm thy fears,—

I 'll lead thee to thy Father-land."

A CHILD OF POVERTY.

THE World hath tried her varied powers
　　To humble this poor, suffering heart,
And deems the blighting of its joys
　　A rich reward for all her art.

I 'd deemed that amaranthine flowers
　　Would bloom perennial round my way,
I wist not that relentless Fate
　　Could turn to night my summer day.

For when I sought with ardent zeal,
　　A cherished object to obtain,
She cast her fetters round my path,
　　And laughed to see my efforts vain.

My lonely heart could not restrain
　　The tears which would unbidden flow,
For all my struggles were in vain ;
　　The false enchantress would not go.

But closer still she drew her coils
　　Around her helpless victim's head,
'Till Hope, which once my life adorned.
　　Seared by her glance, lay cold and dead.

Then Wealth, in gaudy plumage sought
　　To crush beneath her golden heel,
A soul, by nature formed too proud,
　　At such a tarnished shrine to kneel.

I saw the tree of Knowledge stand
　　In wisdom's garden, and I dare
Presume to pluck its cherished fruit ;
　　But Fate's keen sword was waving there.

She bade me leave those classic bowers,

    To dwell 'neath uncongenial skies,—

A cluster of the choicest fruit

    From off the tree, my only prize.

I longed to mingle with the wise,

    The good, the noble, and the pure,

Alas, I had no golden key

    To spring the bolt which closed their door.—

For they had caught the canker blight

    Which deems wealth, merit's corner-stone,

And rather chill, than warm with smiles,

    A genius equal to their own.

But there *are* souls earth cannot crush,

    Though they they may feel each bitter sting,

And genius, tuned by sorrow's key,

    Doth higher soar, and sweeter sing.

"SONGS IN THE NIGHT."

"SONGS in the night!" O, Savior,
    The night so long and drear,
The blessed promise brightens,—
    The promised song doth cheer.

We're listening for their music
    Amid the nations din,—
The panic, crime, and sorrow—
    The turmoil, strife, and sin.

Anon we catch the echoes,
    As the holy songs resound
A golden thread of harmony,
    Amid the discord found.

The night is dark ; but grandly
    From Bethlehem's plain there rolls
The glorious anthem swelling
    With peace, for weary souls.

Each heart prolongs the chorus
    From mountain, hill, and plain,
Till earth, responsive, echoes
    The anthem back again.

7

DELIVERANCE WILL COME.

"DELIVERANCE will come!" sang the loved
  ones at even;
I heard the sweet promise—I claimed it as mine;
Though old, yet 'twas new—'twas a message from
  heaven,
  Which flooded my soul with a rapture divine.

"Deliverance will come!" sad and long have I waited,
  While measuring years by the throbbings of pain;
Bowing my head till the tempest abated,
  Hoping and waiting for rescue in vain.

Waiting for Him—for the Lord who delivers;
  Waiting for Him who is mighty to save;

Waiting in anguish while every nerve quivers;
  Asking for patience and grace to be brave.

Far into night hath my vigil been keeping;
  Long, long ago did the last star decline;
Weary of watching while comrades are sleeping,
  Father, I'm waiting deliverance divine.

Weary thy child, to Thy bosom I'm fleeing;
  Dark is the way; in my weakness I come,
Grant me *one* star my lone pathway revealing;
  Guide and deliver, and welcome me home.

" Deliverance will come!" still their chorus repeating;
  I queried (as faintly I joined the refrain)
Should it come only when heart-strings are breaking,
  Will the seed-time of sorrow prove fruitless and vain?

Fruitless and vain? 'Tis through great tribulation
  The ransomed of earth to the Father must go;

Then welcome the trials, the grief, the temptation,

Hereafter their mission of love we shall know.

" Deliverance will come ! " still the anthem is ringing,

Faith catches the song and re-echoes the strain ;

Though weary the night, the morning is bringing

Deliverance from sorrow, from anguish and pain.

"MIGHT HAVE BEEN."

———, Thou art the cherished one
    Who ope'd for me the gates of love;
No other had its bolts removed,—
    No other waked the slumbering dove.

My heart doth revel in the glow
    Thy love doth shed around my way;
Thy gentle voice in accents mild
    Doth crown with joy each passing day.

The seven years together spent,
    Seem like a sweet—a blissful dream;
Or, like the ripple of the wave,
    Which marks the current of the stream.
7*

'Twas with a maiden's timid trust
  I gave my heart and hand to you;
The future all an unknown path;
  The past, in duty, sealed from view.

But as the years passed swiftly on
  I joyed to find my trust secure;
The love undimmed by seven years,
  Will to the end unchanged endure.

Around the strong protecting oak
  How gently doth the ivy twine,
So with the tendrils of my heart
  Thy love doth mingle, and combine.

Our Father's smile hath blessed our vows;
  His love has hallowed every hour,
His spirit shall our footsteps lead
  To heaven's fair and fadeless bower.

There love divine will shed its ray,

    Around our hearts' entwined in one ;

While hand in hand we join the song,

    Which echoes round the Father's throne.

"MARIAN."

"UP where the pearls of the heavenly portal
   Crown the still waters so goldenly sweet,
Wilt thou not wreathe me a garland immortal,
   Like to the lilies that grow at thy feet?
Marian, Marian, sorrow is clinging
   Round my lone heart, like the shadows of even;
Teach me the song that the angels are singing,
   Smile on my soul from the gateway of heaven."

                                    Annie Herbert.

MARIAN'S REPLY.

A zephyr hath borne to my ear thy sad wailing,
   Thou dearest companion of life's sunny hours,
And, if an immortal, still deem not unheeding
   Thy Marian, lost to earth's mystical bowers.

Gone before, safe at rest, now, in Heaven, I wait thee,

    Where *waiting* is only an anthem sublime,

With never a minor refrain in its echo—

    Never a wail with our melodies chime.

Annie, dear Annie, rejoice in thy sorrow,

    'Twill prove but the passport to joys unrevealed ;

The dark cloud of sadness may vanish to-morrow—

    To glory immortal thine eyes be unsealed.

I twine thee a wreath formed of lilies immortal—

    A garland resplendent with lustre divine—

To circle thy brow, ere you enter the portal

    Which severs our mystical union with Time ;—

Patience, to bear all the ills that beset you ;

    Grace, to subdue all the evil within ;

Faith, to secure every joy that awaits thee ;

    Hope, the sure anchor of glory, to win.

Annie, dear Annie, the harp-notes are ringing,

    Grandly sublime, through the home of the blest ;—

This is the song that the ransomed are singing :

    " Glory to God for salvation, and rest."

Think not unheeded the thorns in thy pathway,

    Bravely removed, or so patiently borne ;

Smiling, I wait thy release from each sorrow

    Which, poignant and bitter, thy spirit hath torn.

I am waiting for thee by Life's calm, flowing River,

    As I stand 'neath Life's Tree, on its beautiful

    shore,—

Waiting to crown thee, with fragrance immortal,

    When we meet in its shade to be severed no more.

Annie, dear Annie, the morning is breaking ;

    Dark was thy night, but its shadows will flee ;

Soon shall I welcome thy spirit immortal,

    Crowned with the blest, on Life's infinite Sea.

MINNIE'S BRIDAL.

They dressed her in white silken robes.
  Each stitch with Love's bright fancies fraught;
And brightest dreams of hope and joy,
  With every thread, her heart had wrought.

And Paul had said: "So fair a gem,
  So rich a setting well may spare;
I've wooed her for her noble soul,
  Her modest worth, her graces rare."

For he had left his city home,
  Vexed with its vanities and pride;
And in this quiet vale had found
  Sweet Minnie Lee, his chosen bride.

This would have been their bridal day;—

   The orange wreath doth crown her brow;—

Why doth she and her train delay?

   The guests are here,—the priest doth wait.

And what a waiting! Lo! they come :

   Ah! see the strong man bowed by grief!

Another claims his darling one,—

   Life gave the bride away to Death!

THE REPROOF.

" WRITE," said the angel, and I wrote
    The happy, joyous dream of youth,
Unsullied by earth's tinsel glare,
    Unstinted in its meed of truth.

The dream, incarnate gaily dressed,
    Within a flower-decked barge I placed,
And launched upon a fairy sea,
    Which Love, and Hope, and Pleasure graced.

The tide, receding, bore them hence,
    The fairy music fainter grew ;
They had no compass, chart, or guide,
    And flowers the Pole-star hid from view.
    8

I heeded not the mild reproof,

    I fancied in the angel's eyes ;

And, in my flowery barge, I left

    My ideal sailing for the skies.

The angel frowned ; in tones severe,

    Reproved me for an erring guide,

Who sought, with flowers, to cover thorns,

    And ocean's storms in caves to hide.

Haste! warn them of Deception's shoals,

    And Passion's tempests that may rise—

Of rocks of doubt and unbelief,

    Which in the calmest water lies.

Write of Temptation's subtle power,

    Of victories over self to gain,

Of crosses to be bravely borne,

    Of resignation born of pain ;

For storms will rise ; the tempest's rage

   May lash life's sea from shore to shore !

Then will thy fairy barque survive

   The surging storm, the billows' roar.

Life is too brief, its needs too vast

   For Reason's sleep, or Fancy's play ;—

A long Eternity awards

   The conquests we achieve to-day.

APRIL TENTH.

SWEET sister mine, how years have fled!
  We're hastening onward to Life's noon;
Nor wait we there, but forward still;—
  We'll view the golden sunset soon.

The sowing-time of life has passed;
  We watch with care the ripening grain;
The harvest in the future waits
  The complement of toil and pain.

Our faith, our patience, and our hope,
  We'll twine around our gathered sheaves;
And thus, before the Master's throne,
  The fruitage of our harvest leave.

To-day you weld another link
  In Life's brief chain, and cheerful press
To greet the duties, joys, and fears,
  That wait you in the wilderness.

Our loving hearts would choose thy path,
  Joyous and bright with song and flowers ;
More wise than we, the God of Love
  May lead, through grief, to Eden's bowers.

But yet we know his way is best,
  And bow, submissive, to his will ;
And, trusting, place our hands in his,
  Through joy or grief, to follow still.

8*

"HE GIVETH SLEEP."

YES, I see the sun declining,
　Shadows lengthen on the way;
Long has been the day, and weary;
　Glad, I hail the evening gray.
Now I lay me down to slumber;
　Savior, guard my sleeping clay.
Let me wake to life immortal
　On the resurrection day.

　　Don't forget to call me, Savior,
　　　From my dreamless couch of clay;
　　Glad, Thy welcome voice I'll answer
　　　On the resurrection day.

While I sleep beneath Death's shadow,
  Where Thy holy dust hath lain,
Thou wilt watch and guard my slumber—
  Thou wilt wake to life again.
Thou art coming, crowned with glory,
  Heaven and earth's triumphant King;
And Thy voice, Thy slumbering children
  From their dusty beds will bring.

    Don't forget *me*, O my Savior !
      Call me early from my clay;
      Clothe me in a garb immortal
      On the resurrection day.

I am weary, fainting, dying,
  Gliding down Death's lonely steep,
Trusting in the blessed promise
  That its shadow is but sleep;

For, to " His beloved He giveth

Sleep," sweet sleep, and rest from pain,

Till the storms of earth are over,

Then to life he'll call again.

Sweet I'll sleep; but in that morning

He will rend my bonds of clay;

Clothed in youth, I'll rise immortal

On the resurrection day.

Farewell, Earth! thy night *so* dreary

Faith has hushed in blissful calm;

In that glorious morn I'll triumph

O'er thy futile power to harm,—

Triumph, through the Savior's merit,

O'er temptation, death and sin,—

Sing His praise, through endless ages,

Who my crown of life did win.

Yes, "He giveth His beloved
  Sleep," to span the lonely way,
Through the dreary realms of shadow,
  To the resurrection day.

BETH.

DON'T think you trouble me,
> If you " swear ; "
For I do not care a straw— ·
> So there !
I have heard your bark before,
And I rather like its roar ;
So treat us to some more—
> If you dare.

I shall send my " dishes old,"
> If I please
I shall " hull corn " again,
> Just to tease

A school-ma'am, rude and rough,
Who goes off in a huff,
If you just send her snuff

For a sneeze.

But, before you begin,

Have a care,
Or the neighbors will think

You on a "tare;"
So, fasten well your door;
Then, in the middle floor,
Open wide your mouth, and roar

Out a "swear."

It just makes me laugh,

When I think
How relieved you will feel;—

What a wink

Of ambition satisfied,—
Of revenge so well applied,—
Of a passion gratified,

                 Without " chink."

Just before you begin,

                 Let me know;

I should like to be present

                 At the show.

When school ma'ams take the stage,
Then comedy will rage,
And a box I will engage

                 While you blow.

DECEMBER THIRTY-FIRST.

OLD Year, is this our parting hour?
  Can no fond words detain thee here?
No magic lend its witching power
  To stay thy flight, and keep thee near?

Why thus impatient to depart,
  Thou last brief link in Memory's chain?
Thy going drapes my soul in gloom,
  And fills my heart with bitter pain.

And yet it is small meed of joy
  That thou hast scattered o'er my way—
Thy fingers swept a broken lyre,
  And thrilled its chords in mournful lay.
  9

'Twas not thy fault that thou didst find
   The broken harp on willows hung,—
A harp thy elder brother's hands
   By harsher play had nigh unstrung.

And still thy younger brother near,
   May prove less kind than they or thou,—
Lay heavier crosses at my feet,—
   With sharper thorns entwine my brow.

I cannot change old friends for new,
   Nor with the cypress twine the palm;
Nor hush the tumult in my breast,
   And quell its tempest into calm.

I know that future years may bring
   Nepenthe in some chalice rare,
And peaceful calm may crown the brow
   Where erst had rested naught but care.

Farewell! Alas, thou goest now
 To join the long procession vast,
Which spans Time's sea from shore to shore,
 And links the future with the past.

Farewell! But list;—we meet again
 When all thy brotherhood have passed
The cycle of the years, and 'waked
 By echoes of the trumpet blast.

Then will I learn your discipline,
 To bless, and purify, was given ;
And every tear, and pain, and woe,
 Its antidote will find in heaven.

LOSS AND GAIN.

THERE is music enthrilling the calm summer air,
    It skims o'er the fringes of thought like a bird ;
Most sweetly it lulls, but it never could rouse ;
    For the depths of the spirit no cadence has heard.

The artist sings on, like the birds at our door,
    Unmeasured the lay, and unnoted the theme ;
No life-blood commingles the song that we hear ;—
    It falls on the ear like a beautiful dream.

Poor heart ! it must pass through the crucible's
    heat—
The furnace of sorrow, of trial, and pain ;—
At the fountain of Marah must linger to drink
    Of its dark, seething waters again and again.

Now, there floats on the air a sweet rapturous lay;
    We listen, entranced, to the soul-stirring strain;
We feel that a spirit is paving our way,
    With its heart's blood and tears, to a loftier plain.

We measure our meed by the notes of the bird,—
    He lays *all* the wealth of his heart at our feet;
The soul of the minstrel, transmuted to song,
    Would lure us from earth by its melody sweet.

The blood-infused poem will live on for aye,
    For the life of the artist is thridding each line;
From the heart's broken chalice alone there can flow
    The fragrance encrypt by the Artist divine.

      *   *.   *   *

A sculptor toiled at the marble block
    From morn till the star-begemmed night,

When his cherished dream, by labor evoked,
     Appeared in its beautiful light.

For only by loss of its prisoning walls,
     Could the skill of the master appear ;
And the vision of youth, in its beauty, at last
     Reward all his labor and care.

So true was he wed to his beautiful art,
     That his strength, life and spirit he gave ;
Then she rose, in her beauty, a monument rare.
     His name for the Future to save.

He lives, and shall live while the ages roll on,
     In the works which his spirit portrayed ;
For creations of genius, immortal as she.
     Were not born, like the author, to fade.

For Art will survive, though the artist decay,
   For works are less transient, less frail than the hand ;
And the life-breathing marble, or flashings of thought,
   Time cannot to darkness remand.

'Twas Art paved the streets of the City of God,
   The foundation laid of its bright jasper wall ;
Its gardens and fountains in beauty arrayed ;
   And painted the rainbow encircling all.

'Twas she swept the harp when the morning stars
   sang—
Her fingers had fashioned its beautiful form ;
Her voice rang the sweetest o'er Bethlehem's plain,
   To herald the tidings—the Savior is born.

On the darkness and gloom of the Edenic night,
   She cast a bright ray o'er the loss we incurred ;

And her spirit still chants through the cycles of time,

That its *loss* will prove *gain* in the Eden restored.

For Art is the breathing of Infinite Love,

And cannot decay, for immortal its birth ;

Immensity, thrilled by its glorious sway,

Is resounding its Architect's praises to earth.

*   *   *   *

On each round we ascend up the ladder of truth,

We must trample some earthly desire ;

For only by *loss* of these clogs do we *gain*

The heaven for which we aspire.

www.ingramcontent.com/pod-product-compliance
Lightning Source LLC
Chambersburg PA
CBHW030547270326
41927CB00008B/1556